following ISBN: 978-1-365-87471-0

THE RETURN OF JESUS CHRIST

By: Leif William

Prologue

This is a book about the coming return soon of the King of the Kings: Jesus Christ just now Jan 2017 almost no time left. The final return of the King: Jesus Christ as the title tells – I begin this book with me as witness of my salvation in Jesus Christ but it is also given prophesies about the near time in front of us. It's a very interesting and giving book. Wish you good reading.

Kind Regards

Leif William

I became a personal Pentecostal Christian the 8th of July 1983 – I went baptized in the grave with Jesus Christ the 20th of September 1987 in Betel Pentecostal Church in Trondheim, Norway and came in touch as early as 1984 with Aage Samuelsen and was in his movement from then he gave me advice to join Pentecostal church of Trondheim – and 15th of November 1987 I got baptized in the Holy Spirit at Aages meeting in turnhallen Oslo – just now I am about to join Pentecostal movement of Norway – central in Oslo by 14th of March 2009. To meet Jesus and God and get salvation be reborn as a Christian is the biggest happening in my life and never will be otherwise – can't ever. End this spelling with these words: None comes to the Father without by Jesus!" And thank you God and Jesus the King and Lord - met God and Jesus and got salvation 8th of July 1983 at a Airport. I became a Pentecostal Christian in 1984 - and Baptized into

Pentecostal Church: Betel the 20th of September 1987 and baptized in Holy Spirit. To get Salvation from Jesus my King and Master is the biggest happening in my life and always will be. Know that the Bible is to 100% the truth - our bible not the catholic bible - but King James bible is God's words the sum of them to human kind and is Holy and the complete truth from beginning to end of the Holy Bible. THE SALVATION FROM JESUS CHRIST IS THE BIGGEST HAPPENING IN POSITIVE REMARK IN MY LIFE AS A WHOLE. I am a Christian since 8th of July 1983. I do not believe that God and Jesus exist and rules - I do KNOW it. I have met them both personally in my spirit in contact with The Holy Spirit. THE SALVATION OF 8TH OF JULY 1983 THE GREATEST HAPPENING IN MY LIFE AS A WHOLE - BUT ALL HOLY SPIRITS WORK AND THEREBY JESUS WORK AND HIS IS ALL THE HONOR - HE WHO HAS ALL POWER IN HEAVEN AND ON EARTH!

I became baptized – barried with Jesus in the baptism in Betel Pentecostal meeting 20th of September 1987 – I became clinically dead in 1983. I became clinically dead as I mention and met God and Jesus. And was of mercy given salvation and reborn on the 8th of July 1983 on Airport on my way Hospital where I should be transported to the department that healed damages I still had on the body - but had until then from the 24th of June been at a Main Hospital for operation – big operation it was and very difficult but very good doctors and they managed against all odds. – but I even became declared dead but was

clinically dead – and was in the death – and met God and Jesus there among other things that did happen – saw my life as on a TV-Screen pass by at first the last that happened was that both God and Jesus were there and they said: “What shall we do with Leif?” It was said more than once. Then all of a sudden I was back to life in the hospital bed:

Singing; ”HOW GREAT THOUGH ARE!” that song a praise song nothing else did fit at all none of the songs from a Agriculture Christian School did fit there and then. And got reborn and got salvation on the 8th of July 1983. And I do know that the whole bible is God’s words and it is true and to be followed and that Jesus is alive and doing that fore us give us salvation – God,

Jesus and Holy spirits work alone. That gods words in the Bible is the complete truth for us and that the Bible is Holy. God met me there and Jesus at the airport the 8th of July 1983 when I said yes: “Jesus come in to my heart I want to be your child!”.

And all of a sudden God’s Holy Spirit filled me complete and God talked Prophetic through me for everyone who was at the airport could hear it was like thunder in the voice I was lying down to be carried in to the ambulance to take me to hospital and the quotes where from the Holy Bible:

“In the last days, God says, I will pour out my Spirit over all people, Your sons and daughters will prophesy, your young men will see visions, you old men will dream dreams. Even on my servants, both men and women. I will pour out my Spirit in those days, and they will prophesy. I will show wonders in the heaven above and signs on the earth below, blood and fire and billows smoke. The sun will be turned to darkness and the moon to blood, before the coming of the great and glorious day of the Lord. And everyone that calls the name of the Lord will be saved.”

I never had read it any place - not read so much as a word from The Bible before that time.

It is written in The Holy Bible in the old Gospel but also in Acts: in Acts repeated of Peter the Rock - and it is also written that it is in the very last times that shall happen - “that God will pour out his Spirit over all people!” - and Pentecostal movement did grow up

because it did happen first time in the USA among poor people there - it was in the year of 1907 it did happen in USA – the prophesy fulfilled and it is in the end of time it shall happen it is written in The Bible. Or as Jesus Christ do say: "In the close of time!". And it will happen very soon that the end do come after that - and now 2008 - 100 years has gone since then - but still we are living in the very last days and the return of Jesus Christ were he shall judge the whole human kind - still living and those who are dead too. And divide evildoers from the righteous. But there is only one way to be named righteous and it is by take Jesus into the heart - no other way there is to salvation. Because only he is to 100% righteous - none else at all. And we are given by mercy righteousness and salvation through Jesus and Holy Spirits work alone so none have any reason to say: I am myself righteous - because none is. Except Jesus and God.

And from Isaiah in the old Gospel quote: "From now I create something new – don't you recognize it? It is already growing up.

Until then I hadn't even read in The Bible of anything of that very little as a matter of fact read in The Bible – but had had a child belief since I was 3 years old. After that I was carried in to the ambulance and got the permission to talk inside me directly to God and Jesus. And I did then say: "What is really this?" "I heard all

the time: non can know God and Jesus do exist! How then this???" Answer: "There is no problem at all knowing that we do exist everyone can know that!".

And in 1984 when I went an Agricultural School – a Christian School – to get to become a Agronom – had gone Pure Agricultural School at first to become a farmer between 1981 and 1982 – at I went to this Agricultural School because I searched after God and

Jesus. I at that time I used to go to each meeting at that School it was a Christian School. But still not got salvation or being born again. One day early in the spring at this School I went out for a walk it was mild temperature outside and no wind at all – it was late in the evening and it was dark. Then I begged in my suffering in longing after knowing if God and Jesus is the truth. "If you are the truth then give me a sign God!" I prayed. All of a sudden in the sky just over the treetops there was lightened up a round light in yellow, I wondered – then another one was lighten up the same way – looked like lights on a car – but up in the sky – and after that a third one; one after the other horizontally three lights in different colours – then a light was shown over that one that was in the middle: Then I thought if one in add now under the others are lightened up – it becomes a cross! all they were in different colours; and it did a fifth light was lightened up so it made a cross showing – very big could almost seems like a airplane was about to crash but the light did stand complete still and I stood watching for a long time. Then I thought maybe it is

a UFO – and then I walked back to the internate – and the belief it was a UFO I did keep fore long time I had seen didn't end believing just that until 1983 8/7 – when God told: "It was a sign from me my child – you begged to me to give you one and it was given!". Is also written in bible beg and you shall be given.

In 1981 to 1984 I got anorexia but God did remove that in one day in 10th of November 1984 – after that never had it – I was only 46 kg and I am 180 cm tall and in 3 weeks I was in normal weight had to eat for three weeks and became 76 kg that is normal and God and Jesus helped my – by his wound you get healthy from sickness is also written. And 8th of July 1983 I got salvation from God and Jesus as mentioned.

When we were on an educational journey at the Agricultural School in 1985 I went to Philadelphia – a Pentecostal church on meeting one day. After that because I was a youth and begun at an education: Office related and became Account Manager in 1988.

In September 1987 I had gone out of the Lutheranian Jew hateress church – this I do say because Luther has written scrips that made almost each country that had Lutheranian belief to be filled with Jew hatetress through history in Europe even used by Hitler those scripts and I wanted to become a member in the Pentecostal movement and be barried in the baptism with Jesus. Then

I phoned to Betel – another Pentecostal church and ask if they could baptize me – complete under the water – as it is done and told in the Bible to do. And The Bible is to a 100% truth that I do know. Also because that I on the 8th of July 1983 when I got salvation from God and Jesus - they spoke through me prophetic quotes from The Holy Bible that I never before in my whole life until then had read or heard at any point. But read it afterwards.

Read much in the Bible after that time and do still do so. Know it is God's Holy word's each inch of it and the complete truth is in it to be told.

I became a personal Pentecostal Christian the 8th of July 1983 – I went baptized in the grave with Jesus Christ the 20th of September 1987 in Betel Pentecostal Church in Trondheim, Norway and came in touch as early as 1984 with Aage Samuelsen and was in his movement from then he gave me advice to join Pentecostal church of Trondheim – and 15th of November 1987 I got baptized in the Holy Spirit at Aages meeting in turnhallen Oslo – just now I am about to join Pentecostal movement of Norway – central in Oslo by 14th of March 2009. To meet Jesus and God and get salvation be reborn as a Christian is the biggest happening in my life and never will be otherwise – can't ever. End this spelling with these words: None comes to the Father without by Jesus!" And thank you God

and Jesus the King and Lord – with all power in Heaven and on earth.

The Pentecostal Movement in Norway was started by Pastor Thomas T. Barratt with a break through in 1907. To day there is about 280 local Pentecostal churches and over 40.000 members. Thomas T. Barrat (Scottish), and Pioneer Aage Samuelsen - both with great importance even worldwide fore Pentecostal church.

It was only a positive attitude and the local movement Pentecostal was blessed with the presence of the Lord himself and the Holy Spirit – after being baptized in Betel I became a member at once – they did write me in at the same time as a member and that I should continue to be until 1990. After this baptism that is urgently necessary for all human beings – there and then it came God spoke through me in Israeli language – ended with I fell on my knees saying Maran-Ata! Maran-Ata! Hallelujah! Hallelujah! The complete ending of it was :"Jesus is here, Jesus is here – Jesus from Nazareth is here." Then it ended. But the same day I was barried with Jesus in the baptism i Betel. I became then a member there the 20th of September 1987.

Pentecostal confession says that bible 100% true and I do know it is the case - I do not believe in God and Jesus I know they are the truth - and Islam most evil organization

on earth and has only to be complete forbidden and removed for all time from earth before

Christ do come back to judge the world - and that is in no time limit just now in July 2008. About 100 years since the mentioned prophesy was fulfilled that is written in Bible and Pentecostal movement came as direct result - and now no time limit left but Islam has to be complete defeated and removed for all time from

earth at first - as criminal organization - if not they anyway got a mighty judgment to meet in no time limit in front of us just now. Also Buddhism and Hinduism and whatever may be just big lies.

But Islam biggest lie - but also the other is lies only – reincarnation never any time happened to anyone is written in The Holy Bible:

“It’s each human beings destiny one time to die and thereafter doom!”.

And that’s clearly words enough just about that matter

itself. But is written also in Bible about Mohammed he is mentioned in revelation of John - Jesus disciple - as: “The false prophet to come!” - what also Islam done - put even a Mosque in Jerusalem and written all around the socket of

that Mosque: "God has no Son!" and that almost worse blaspheme ever occur and should be removed that mosque from Jerusalem for all time to come as fast as possible. Should been done very fast. And what happen everyone has to face Jesus after death and then be judged no matter whom and two possible results of these doom then end up in Heaven of Hell - no other way is. And Jesus say himself: "None do come to the Father without through me!" - also written:

"There is no other name ever mentioned to get salvation through then God's son Jesus!".

Paul says that in Bible. And I know there are no other way for anyone no matter what has of belief on earth all meet Jesus after death - all happen to everyone no exception – no way ever to escape from that: "One time to die thereafter doom" is as mentioned written in bible and know it is true. Islam really bad religion - as a matter of fact no religion at all - just a criminal organization - one of the biggest lies ever told - only Christianity is the complete truth - nothing else - Jesus is the truth in person himself - no matter what humans may believe there are only one real truth and this truth is Jesus Christ himself none else - this I really not believe I know it - and not difficult at all in world of today to know just that – for instance just take a look at the Corp. sheet of Torino and what is found out about it - no leave for doubt then - even Jesus said: "I shall give you only one sign after me: The

Jonah Sign!" - That was in itself that he did rise from death to life and is the only King ruling and got all power in Heaven and on

earth - this is the truth and Bible is truth all of it - God's words it is - spoken to humanity given them as a treasure and a gift – until Jesus do return and will judge all humankind - what Islam concern will get a very hard doom by Christ no doubt either ever to have in that matter - but we humans can even have it forbidden to exist on earth because it as organization brakes almost all of UN's declaration of human rights and that's only fact - truly they soon going to face reality all of them and everyone who do die cause they all are set to face Christ himself without exception... Because he has always been the only truth..

This is the final prophesies I have got the latest as late as now in Nov. 2008 explanation from God and Jesus my King and master – always been – and no other way ever been – this book explains a whole lot about what non did understand when it all happened historically some of historical events that already been.

The Victory of UK in Napolion war against the Fascist Napolion – made a turning point it made the last time all described in bible already all was given then to human king to understand last time – the end of the end. 2000 years ago done and even more then that but completed bible 2000 years ago but not until King James Bible was created by God and Jesus and therefore set an eternal sign on it itself if broken eternal harm just happen – as punishment anyone touch that word – it itself is Holy. The catholic bible is not at all God's word as told in this book and also in earlier books in this matter: The Catholic church is the bitch in revelation book – the rest of the parts in revelation book is to be explain in this book all of them – it is soon the end of all time therefore now do it: Was told me by met God and Jesus first time: 8th of July 1983 – 4 days after USA's independence day it was – what also happen historically that make prophesies fulfilled is second world war all told in Daniel in detail about it: easy to see it and Jesus do also say: "The one who have eyes and want do understand this!". All parts in end time prophesies is explained in this book itself – no more need now for me to add in this matter – and Russia also was something USSR was the Gog and Magog told in Bible several places. As an evil Empire. And Armangeddon to come in war against them it was the cold war.

"And I saw, and behold a white horse: and he that sat on him had a bow; and a crown was given unto him: and he

went forth conquering, and to conquer. And I saw heaven opened, and behold a white horse; and he that sat upon him was called Faithful and True, and in righteousness he doth judge and make war. And the He fought against the False Prophet at last - and the False Prophet was thrown in Gahenna... And the rest of them were all killed with the sword of fire in the hand by King riding the white horse. Then I saw a great white throne and the King of Kings was seated on and crowned he is and - and each person was judged according to what they had done.... And the devil was town into the lake of eternal fire and eternal suffer... The death and Hades were thrown in the lake of fire... And if anyone's name was not found, he was thrown into the lake of fire and eternal suffer forever divided from God's people.

Quote: Matthew: Jesus Christ: "So don't be afraid of them. There are nothing hidden that will not be disclosed, or hidden that will not be made known. What I do tell you in the dark, speak it in daylight; what is whispered in your ear, proclaim it from the roofs!" "I did not come to bring peace, but a sword. For it I come to turn!" "If anyone won't welcome you or listen to your words, shake the dust off your feet; when you leave that home or town. I tell you truly; it will be more bearable fore Sodom and Gomorrah on the Day of Judgment then fore that town."

Quotes from The Holy Bible: In the beginning God created created man and woman and said to them it took seven

days for Him to create what he had decided – the first he created was light the first word from God word was: Let there be light! And the light should become the humans light and it is also named the word – but the darkness did not welcome him – but all those who did welcome him he gave the right to become God's children. The light became man – and born to earth – and the light is the only word also mentioned at and the word it a man – and is created in God's picture but also a part of God – God is one Holy God – and the name of the word is: Jesus Christ – the King of the Kings he who now rules Heaven and Earth. The only name getting salvation from is through the name: Jesus – no other. He is the only truth he is the only: way, the truth and even is the life itself – without him not possible get eternal life for any human being only through Christ given salvation no other way. When man and woman finally was created the 7th day – God was pleased with all His creation and said: "Everything is now good!" – It will with other words say: Everything is now perfect the way it is.

"After the death sin done by Adam and Eve – by being told to do so by the Devil – is the Garden of Eden in Israel – it was told by God you can eat fruit of all the trees in the Garden with exception only one if you do so you shall die."

It did happen about 6000 years ago and no could after that be more then1000 years or 1 day it is for God – and none should ever be one day or 1000 years old.

And it is written: "It is the human beings destiny one time to die – thereafter doom!" – but Christ came to rescue the human kind cause it was not possible to get saved without

He do Gods will in all parts – and he did on behalf of all human kind – and he did die on the cross and there after he was risen from death by God after three days. There and then in Israel by a Jew – the rescue of human kind the possibility fore was reality now about 2000 years ago. God's mercy alone gives salvation by believing in Jesus and no other way there are – never been and never shall be until the close of age.

**"When the Son of man comes in his glory, and all the
angels with him, then he will sit on his glorious throne. 32
Before him will be gathered all the nations, and he will
separate them one from another as a shepherd separates
the sheep from the goats, 33 and he will place the sheep
at his right hand, but the goats at the left. 34 Then the
King will say to those at his right hand, 'Come, O blessed
of my Father, inherit the kingdom prepared for you from
the foundation of the world; 35 for I was hungry and you
gave me food, I was thirsty and you gave me drink, I was a
stranger and you welcomed me, 36 I was naked and you
clothed me, I was sick and you visited me, I was in prison
and you came to me.' 37 Then the righteous will answer
him, 'Lord, when did we see thee hungry and feed thee, or
thirsty and give thee drink? 38 And when did we see thee
a stranger and welcome thee, or naked and clothe thee?
39 And when did we see thee sick or in prison and visit
thee?' 40 And the King will answer them, 'Truly, I say to
you, as you did it to one of the least of these my brethren,
you did it to me.' 41 Then he will say to those at his left
hand, 'Depart from me, you cursed, into the eternal fire
prepared for the devil and his angels; 42 for I was hungry**

and you gave me no food, I was thirsty and you gave me no drink, 43 I was a stranger and you did not welcome me, naked and you did not clothe me, sick and in prison and you did not visit me.' 44 Then they also will answer, 'Lord, when did we see thee hungry or thirsty or a stranger or naked or sick or in prison, and did not minister to thee?' 45 Then he will answer them, 'Truly, I say to you, as you did it not to one of the least of these, you did it not to me.' 46 And they will go away into eternal punishment, but the righteous into eternal life."

How it all happened that what Jesus had said: "The whole and complete truth shall set you all free!"

Albert Einstein told: "I prove everything there is" And even prove mathematic that God and Jesus and Holy Spirit is true – scientifically prove – he did that in USA and all his work was save by USA and most parts now in pentagon.

THE END OF THE END THE EMPIRE OF JESUS CHIRST TO COME - SOON!

"And I saw a Beast coming out of sea.... That beast was killed and thrown in the Lake of fire and by the King riding the white horse – but is then following setting "And then I saw another beast, coming out of the earth" – the power the last beast has it takes from the first – and the King riding the white horse did destroy also this last beast and throw it all in the lake of fire where the first beast already is and Antichrist also just one thing left then to take the beast that came out of earth and then create the complete

work – command to do so by Jesus Christ – at last after the doom set. The King on the white horse: Jesus Christ - by command: "Devide et impera" – then this little part – the little beast on earth be all thrown in Hell and creation of Hell for all evil creatures to be for all time in eternal pain and punishment – no ever end of it when the last beast killed and the Devil who do rules that last location as a country or a city be determinated for all time all of it fore all time to come by the sword of fire in the hand of the King of Kings Jesus Christ. " "Concerning the coming of the Lord Jesus Christ , that day will not come until the rebellion occurs and the man of lawlessness is revealed, the man doomed to destruction. He will oppose and will exalt himself over that is named God or us worshipped - and even proclaim himself to be God!" "And now you can know who is holding him back, so he may be revealed at the proper time. For the secret power of the lawlessness is already at work. And then the lawless one will be revealed; whom the Lord Jesus will overthrow complete - determinate. The grace of our Lord Jesus Christ be with you all and defend you in the power of God's Holy Spirit. (2 Thes. 2)Then only one word left for the King to say: "The Heavenly Kingdom is now completed and it is just fore you be children and to take part of your heritage that been prepared for you before the creation itself!" And at very last Jesus then will say one setting. "The Heavenly kingdom of the King Jesus Christ is now closed!" to be ruled by him the everlasting Heavenly Empire with Iron hand for all time – no end no beginning really had. God and Jesus always has ruled all there is. "

"And soon our King Jesus Christ is going return to judge all flesh – all human kind as King and judge at judgment day – when he do close the age and we the Kingdom of Heaven for all eternity. The New Jerusalem to inherit fore eternity to come no end of it. And meet all our beloved ones there. Then the King of Kings will say: Now the time is closed! God bless you all here mentioned and who is not none forgotten. God bless the USA – the Heavenly Kingdom to come very soon in no time limit. Jesus Christ's Heavenly final Empire to be ruled by iron hand and mercy fore all time to come. Very soon now Jesus is going to return and that is the end of the end.".

"From now I God create something new - you shall not be able to say this I knew from before - but don't you see it you can all do so it is already growing up..."

THAT IS THE END OF THE END AFTER THAT THE STARS SHALL FALL DOWN FROM HEAVEN AND SUN TURN AWAY AND MOON TOO - AND THE SIGN OF JESUS CHRIST THE HOLY CROSS WILL APPEAR IN THE SKY. THEN JESUS CHRIST COMES VISIABLE FORE ALL FLESH AND THE PARADISE THEN AFTER THE DOOM BE REALITY FORE ALL TIME. THAT IS THE WHOLE STORY TO COME IN NEAR FUTURE. NO TIME LIMIT ALMOST. "FIRE!" A VERY OLD EXPRESSION AND COMMAND IS SOUNDING JUST NOW BY OUR LORD JESUS CHRIST HIM SELF: IT IS THE VERY LAST COMMAND IN THIS AND IS A COMMAND DIRECTED TO GOD'S AND JESUS HEAVENLY KINGDOM THE USA JUST NOW. GOD WILL ALWAYS ETERNELY BLESS THE USA AND ISRAEL! THEY ARE BOTH TOGETHER THE UNITED STICK IN GOD'S HAND. (COMPARE EZ. 37 AND SO ON). GOD BLESS AMERICA AND ISRAEL AND THE EXPRESSION BE TRUE: "STARS AND STRIPES FORE EVER!" - NO EVER END OF IT NOT EVER. AMEN. THE GRACE OF OUR LORD JESUS CHRIST BLESS THOSE TWO NATIONS FORE ALL TIME TO COME. ETERNELY. GOD'S AND JESUS HEAVENLY KINGDOM. GOD BLESS USA AND ISRAEL! JESUS CHRIST OUR LORD IS UNDER RETURN AND WILL CLOSE THE TIME AND THE HEAVENLY KINGDOM FORE GOD'S CHILDREN TO INHERIT NOW VERY

SOON. JUST SOME FEW PARTS LEFT IN ALL PROPHESIES GIVEN IN HOLY BIBLE LEFT. AND JUST WAIT NOW FORE ONE FINAL COMMAND FROM OUR LORD JESUS CHRIST HIM SELF THE COMMAND: FIRE! AFTER THAT FINAL COMMAND - ALL THE AGES BE CLOSED BY JESUS CHRIST HIM SELF AS HE HAS PROMISED TO DO THEN. "AND LOOK I AM WITH YOU ALL THE AGES UNTIL I CLOSE THE AGE!" QUOTE: JESUS CHRIST MATTHEW.

At last God bless Pentecostal movement world wide and Pentecostal churches of New York and Florida and the United States. And as last adding God and Jesus Christ bless Pentecostal Church of Oslo, Norway were I am a member – and Norway's Pentecostal movement country wide.

IN EZRAS 4RD BOOK IN JEWISH BIBLE IS TOLD THAT ALL ANIMALS IN BIBLE ARE EITHER EMPIRES OR COUNTRIES. AND HAS THERE BEEN ANY GREATER EMPIRE ON EARTH THEN THE USA? ONLY ASK. SOMETHING HAPPENED ALSO BACK IN 1907 IN AZUSA IN USA THE FOUNDATION OF THE PENTECOSTAL MOVEMENT. AFTER GOD LET HIS SPIRIT POUR OUT OVER ALL FLESH THERE. AS PROPHESIES GIVEN ABOUT THE LAST TIME BEFORE JESUS CHRIST HIM SELF CLOSE THE AGE. "AND I AM WITH YOU TILL THE CLOSE OF AGE!" - NOW TO SOME

QUOTES FROM THE HOLY BIBLE TO CONFIRM AND SOME WRITING FROM A BOOK OF MINE NAMED BIBLE ADD:

For as the lightning comes from the east and shines as far as the west, so will be the coming of the Son of man. Wherever the body is, there the eagles will be gathered together. Immediately after the tribulation of those days the sun will be darkened, and the moon will not give its light, and the stars will fall from heaven, and the powers of the heavens will be shaken; then will appear the sign of the Son of man in heaven, and then all the tribes of the earth will mourn, and they will see the Son of man coming on the clouds of heaven with power and great glory; and he will send out his angels with a loud trumpet call, and they will gather his elect from the four winds, from one end of heaven to the other.

"When the Son of man comes in his glory, and all the angels with him, then he will sit on his glorious throne. Before him will be gathered all the nations, and he will separate them one from another as a shepherd separates the sheep from the goats, and he will place the sheep at his right hand, but the goats at the left. Then the King will say to those at his right hand, "Come, O blessed of my Father, inherit the kingdom prepared for you from the foundation of the world; for I was hungry and you gave me food, I was thirsty and you gave me drink, I was a stranger and you welcomed me, I was naked and you clothed me, I was sick and you visited me, I was in prison and you came to me." Then the righteous will answer him, "Lord, when

did we see the hungry and feed thee, or thirsty and give thee drink? And when did we see thee a stranger and welcome thee, or naked and clothe thee? And when did we see thee sick or in prison and visit thee?" And the King will answer them, "Truly, I say to you, as you did it to one of the least of these my brethren, you did it to me." Then he will say to those at his left hand, "Depart from me, you cursed, into the eternal fire prepared for the devil and his angels; for I was hungry and you gave me no food, I was thirsty and you gave me no drink, I was a stranger and you did not welcome me, naked and you did not clothe me, sick and in prison and you did not visit me." Then they also will answer, "Lord, when did we see thee hungry or thirsty or a stranger or naked or sick or in prison, and did not minister to thee?" Then he will answer them, 'Truly, I say to you, as you did it not to one of the least of these, you did it not to me." And they will go away into eternal punishment, but the righteous into eternal life."

“And I saw, and behold a white horse: and he that sat on him had a bow; and a crown was given unto him: and he went for conquering, and to conquer. And I saw heaven opened, and behold a white horse; and he that sat upon him was called Faithful and True, and in righteousness he doth judge and make war. And the He fought agains the False Prophet at last - and the False Prophet was thrown in Gahenna... And the rest of them were all killed with the sword of fire in the hand by the King riding the white horse. Then I saw a great white throne and the King of

Kings was seated on and crowned he is - and each person was jugded according to what they had done.... And the devil was thrown into the lake of eternal fire and eternal suffer... Then death and Hades were thrown in the lake of fire... And if anyone's name was not found, he was thrown into the lake of fire and eternal suffer forever devided from God's people..."

Quote: Matthew: Jesus Christ: "So don't be affraid of them. There are nothing conceailed that will not be disclosed, or hidden that will not be made known. What I do tell you in the dark, speak it in daylight; what is whispered in your ear, proclaim it from the roofs!" "I did not come to bring peace, but a sword. For it I come to turn!" "If anyone won't welcome you or listen your words, shake the dust off your feet; when you leave that home or town. I tell you truly; it will be more bearable fore Sodom and Gomorrah on the day of judgement then fore that town."

Quotes from The Holy Bible.

In the beginning God created man and woman and it took seven days for Him to create what he had decided – the first he created was light the first word from God was: Let there be light! And the light should become the humans light and it is also named the word – but the darkness did not welcome him – but all those who did welcome him he

gave the right to become God's children. The light became man – and born to earth – and the light is the only word also mentioned as and the word is a man – and is created in God's picture but also a part of God – God is one Holy God – and the name of the word is: Jesus Christ – the King of the Kings he who now rules Heaven and Earth. The only name getting salvation from is through the name: Jesus – no other. He is the only truth he is the only: way, the truth and even is the life itself – without him not possible get eternal life for any human being only through Christ given salvation no other way. When man and woman finally was created the 7th day – God was pleased with all His creation and said: "Everything is now good!" – It will with other words say: Everything is now perfect the way it is.

"After the death sin done by Adam and Eve – by being told to do so by the Devil – in the Garden of Eden in Israel – it was told by God you can eat fruit of all the trees in the Garden with exception only one if you do so you shall die."

It did happen about 6000 years ago and none could after that be more than 1000 years or 1 day it is fore God – and none should ever be one day or 1000 years old.

And it is written: "It is the human beings destiny one time to die – there after doom!" – but Christ came to resque the

human kind cause it was not possible to get saved without He do God's will in all parts – and he did on behalf of all human kind – and he did die on the cross and there after he was risen from death by God after three days. There and then in Israel by a Jew – the rescue of human kind the possibility fore was reality now about 2000 years ago. God's mercy alone gives salvation by believing in Jesus and no other way there is – never been and never shall be until the close of age.

"All authority in heaven and on earth has been given to me. Go therefore and make disciples of all nations, baptizing them in the name of the Father and of the Son and of the Holy Spirit, teaching them to observe all that I have commanded you; and lo, I am with you always, to the close of the age."

"For as the lightning comes from the east and shines as far as the west, so will be the coming of the Son of man. Wherever the body is, there the eagles will be gathered together." "Immediately after the tribulation of those days the sun will be darkened, and the moon will not give its light, and the stars will fall from heaven, and the powers of the heavens will be shaken; then will appear the sign of the Son of man in heaven, and then all the tribes of the earth will mourn, and they will see the Son of man coming on the clouds of heaven with power and great glory; and he will send out his angels with a loud trumpet call, and they will gather his elect from the four winds, from one

end of heaven to the other. "From the fig tree learn its lesson: as soon as its branch becomes tender and puts forth its leaves, you know that summer is near. So also, when you see all these things, you know that he is near, at the very gates. Truly, I say to you, this generation will not pass away till all these things take place. Heaven and earth will pass away, but my words will not pass away." "But of that day and hour no one knows, not even the angels of heaven, nor the Son, but the Father only. As were the days of Noah, so will be the coming of the Son of man. For as in those days before the flood they were eating and drinking, marrying and giving in marriage, until the day when Noah entered the ark, and they did not know until the flood came and swept them all away, so will be the coming of the Son of man."

"When the Son of man comes in his glory, and all the angels with him, then he will sit on his glorious throne. Before him will be gathered all the nations, and he will separate them one from another as a shepherd separates the sheep from the goats, and he will place the sheep at his right hand, but the goats at the left. Then the King will say to those at his right hand, "Come, O blessed of my Father, inherit the kingdom prepared for you from the foundation of the world; for I was hungry and you gave me food, I was thirsty and you gave me drink, I was a stranger and you welcomed me, I was naked and you clothed me, I was sick and you visited me, I was in prison and you came to me." Then the righteous will answer him, "Lord, when

did we see thee hungry and feed thee, or thirsty and give thee drink? And when did we see thee a stranger and welcome thee, or naked and clothe thee? And when did we see thee sick or in prison and visit thee?" And the King will answer them, 'Truly, I say to you, as you did it to one of the least of these my brethren, you did it to me." Then he will say to those at his left hand, "Depart from me, you cursed, into the eternal fire prepared for the devil and his angels; for I was hungry and you gave me no food, I was thirsty and you gave me no drink, I was a stranger and you did not welcome me, naked and you did not clothe me, sick and in prison and you did not visit me." Then they also will answer, "Lord, when did we see thee hungry or thirsty or a stranger or naked or sick or in prison, and did not minister to thee?" Then he will answer them, 'Truly, I say to you, as you did it not to one of the least of these, you did it not to me.And they will go away into eternal punishment, but the righteous into eternal life."

How it all happened that what Jesus had said:

“The whole and complete truth shall set you all free!"

And soon our King Jesus Christ is going return to judge all flesh – all human kind as King and judge at judgment day – when he do close the age and we the Kingdom of Heaven fore all eternity. The New Jerusalem to inherit fore eternity to come no end of it. And meet all our beloved

ones there. Then the King of Kings will say: Now the time is closed! God bless you all here mentioned and who is not none forgotten. God bless the USA – the Heavenly Kingdom to come very soon in no time limit. Jesus Christ's Heavenly final Empire to be ruled for all time to come. Very soon now Jesus is going to return and that is the end of the end.

"And I saw, and behold a white horse: and he that sat on him had a bow; and a crown was given unto him: and he went forth conquering, and to conquer. And I saw heaven opened, and behold a white horse; and he that sat upon him was called Faithful and True, and in righteousness he doth judge and make war. And the He fought agains the False Prophet at last - and the False Prophet was thrown in Gahenna... And the rest of them were all killed with the sword of fire in the hand by King riding the white horse. Then I saw a great white throne and the King of Kings was seated on and crowned he is and - and each person was jugded according to what they had done.... And the devil was thrown into the lake of eternal fire and eternal suffer... Then death and Hades were thrown in the lake of fire... And if anyone's name was not found, he was thrown into the lake of fire and eternal suffer forever devided from God's people..."

Quote: Matthew: Jesus Christ: "So don't be affraid of them. There are nothing conceailed that will not be disclosed, or hidden that will not be made known. What I

do tell you in the dark, speak it in daylight; what is whispered in your ear, proclaim it from the roofs!" "I did not come to bring peace, but a sword. For it I come to turn!" "If anyone won't welcome you or listen your words, shake the dust off your feet; when you leave that home or town. I tell you truely; it will be more bearable fore Sodom and Gomorrah on the day of judgement then fore that town."

Quotes from The Holy Bible.

End this book with add God bless the United States of America for eternity. And soon our King Jesus Christ is going return to judge all flesh – all human kind as King and judge at judgment day – when he do close the age and we the Kingdom of Heaven for all eternity. The New Jerusalem to inherit fore eternity to come no end of it. And meet all our beloved ones there. Then the King of Kings will say: Now the time is closed!

THE END

www.ingramcontent.com/pod-product-compliance
Ingram Content Group UK Ltd.
Pitfield, Milton Keynes, MK11 3LW, UK
UKHW041902190726
13854UKWH00003B/1035

9 781365 874710